For Julie Danielson

Dial Books for Young Readers
An imprint of Penguin Random House LLC
1745 Broadway, New York, New York 10019

First published in the United States of America by Dial Books for Young Readers, an imprint of Penguin Random House LLC, 2025
Copyright © 2025 by Jerrold Connors

Dial & colophon are registered trademarks of Penguin Random House LLC.
The Penguin colophon is a registered trademark of Penguin Books Limited.
Visit us online at PenguinRandomHouse.com.
Library of Congress Cataloging-in-Publication Data is available.
ISBN 9780593859346
1 3 5 7 9 10 8 6 4 2
Manufactured in China
TOPL

This book was edited by Jessica Dandino Garrison, copyedited and proofread by Regina Castillo, and designed by Jennifer Kelly. The production was supervised by Jayne Ziemba, Nicole Kiser, and Hansi Weedagama.

The illustrations for this book were drawn in ink with a Winsor and Newton Series 7 Kolinsky sable brush and colored with Kuretake Gansai Tambi watercolors. The artist added digital enhancements in Procreate with the Adilson Farias watercolor brush set. Text set in Adobe Garamond Pro.

This is a work of nonfiction. Some names and identifying details have been changed.

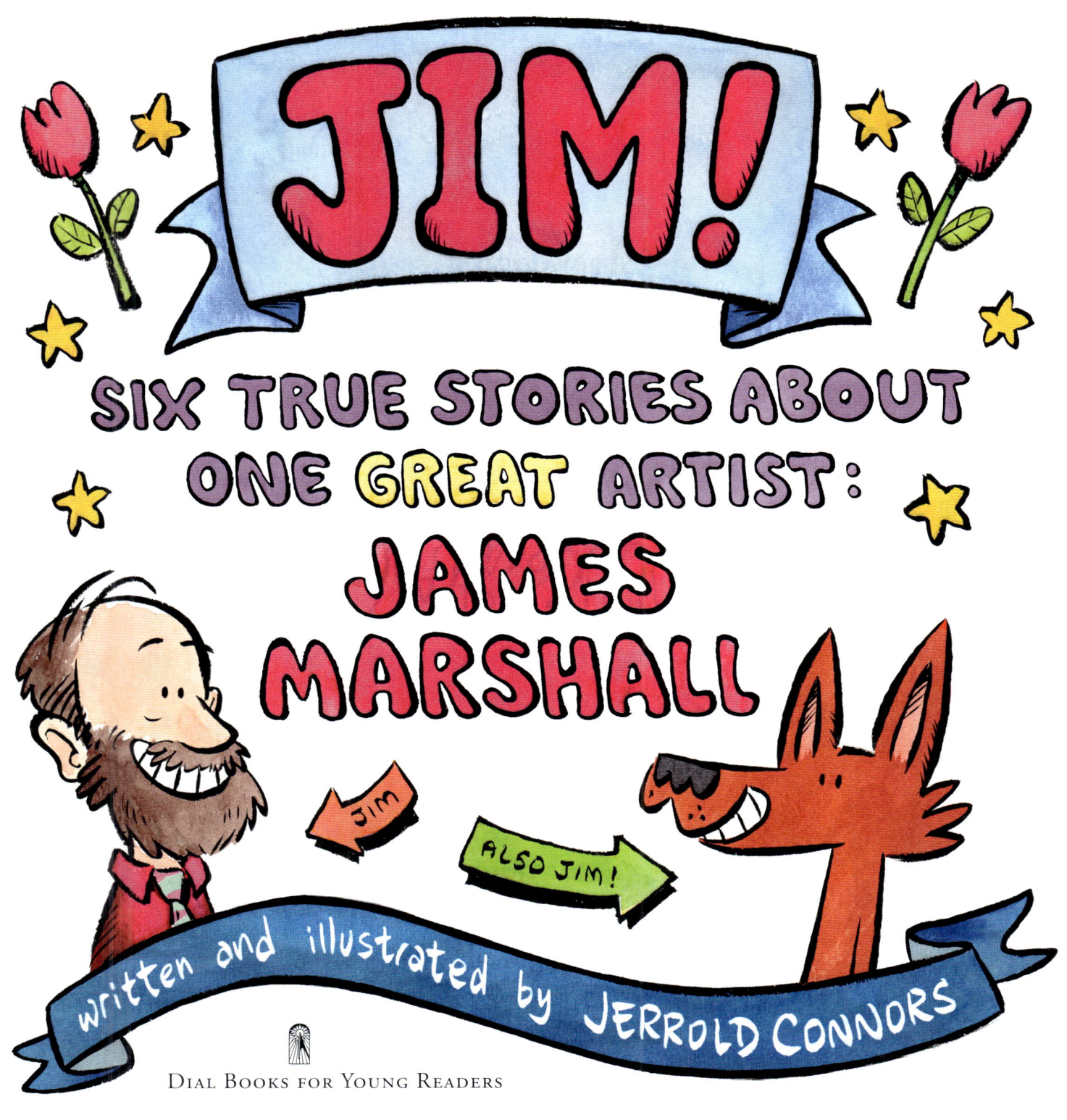

JIM!

SIX TRUE STORIES ABOUT ONE GREAT ARTIST: JAMES MARSHALL

JIM

ALSO JIM!

written and illustrated by JERROLD CONNORS

DIAL BOOKS FOR YOUNG READERS

STORY NUMBER ONE

THE BOOK

James Marshall had a friend named Harry.

Harry was full of wild ideas.

One night Harry called on the telephone.

"Jim," whispered Harry. "Miss Nelson is missing!"

"Interesting," said Jim.

The next day Harry came for a visit.

"Miss Nelson is a teacher," he explained. "She goes missing. But there is a mean substitute teacher and a jealous principal. The school is haunted! And there's a circus sideshow and gargoyles and time travel! Here—I wrote it all down," said Harry.

"I'll have a look," said Jim.

Jim collected the papers and went inside his studio. He took out his pen and made some sketches. In no time, he had whipped Harry's story into shape.

"I like this substitute teacher," he said.
"I have *just* the name for her."

Months later, the story became a bestselling book.

"We sure wrote a good story, didn't we?" said Harry.

"I couldn't have done it without you," said Jim.

STORY NUMBER TWO
"HOW CUTE!"

REVIEWS

James Marshall makes CUTE books.
—A. Critic

People liked James Marshall's books.

"How cute!" they would say about his drawings. Jim did not like that word.

"How zany!" others would say. He liked that word even less.

"You know who never gets called cute or zany?" said Jim. "Classical musicians."

Jim dug out his old viola and started practicing. He liked classical music—it made him feel sophisticated and smart—but he soon realized he liked drawing more.

Jim put the viola away for good.

"I heard you used to be a classical musician," said a fan one day. "Why on earth did you stop?"

Jim thought.

"I . . . um . . . hurt my wrist," he said. "In a terrible plane crash."

"It's a good thing you didn't hurt it badly enough to stop drawing," said a man named Billy, who was browsing books nearby.

"Ah. Yes," said Jim. "It was a lucky accident."

Jim and Billy began to spend time together.

They liked each other quite a lot.

STORY NUMBER THREE
FRIENDLY COMPETITION

James Marshall had two friends who also wrote books.

They were Maurice and Arnold.

Together, the three friends had wild adventures. It was a competition to see who could be the most outrageous.

"Honestly," said Arnold's wife, Anita, "you three are real characters!"

"I can use that!" said Jim.

He began writing another set of books—about a group of rambunctious friends.

"These stories are very good," said Maurice.

"Big deal," said Jim. "I could write a thousand stories and they wouldn't be as beautiful as yours."

"Maybe," said Maurice. "But I could write a *million* stories and they wouldn't be as *funny* as yours."

"Great," said Jim. "You're wiser than me too."

THE AWARD

James Marshall wrote sixty-nine books. Some people still called his art cute.

"It would be nice to get an award," said Jim. "Then maybe people would call my art *great*."

"All great art has something of its creator in it," mused Billy.

"I was born in Texas and I've put *that* in almost all my books,"
 said Jim.

"True," said Billy.

"I've put this self-portrait in most of them as well!" Jim added.

"Handsome fellow," said Billy.

"What else could I add?!" fumed Jim.

"You'll think of it," said Billy.

That night, Jim did a lot of thinking.

The next day, he began painting. He had never put so much of himself into his art.

"There," said Jim finally. "This is going in my next book!"

When Billy saw the book, he smiled.

"This is really good," he said to Jim. "Do you think it will win an award?"

"You know . . ." said Jim. "The thought completely slipped my mind."

"But I wouldn't say no to just *one*."

STORY NUMBER FIVE

THE SCHOOL VISIT

James Marshall was visiting an elementary school. The kids were very excited.

"Quiet, please!" said a teacher.

"Raise your hands!" said another.

"We have time for one last question!" said a third.

A little girl in the front row raised her hand.

"What do you like most about making books?" she asked.

"Let me tell you," said Jim.

"When I was in second grade, I drew a picture of a lovely pecan tree. I thought it was quite good."

"My teacher, however, felt differently.

'Jimmy,' she said, 'You will never be an artist.'"

"BOOOOO!!!" shouted the kids.

"Many years later my friend Harry and I wrote a book together. I needed a villainous character, so I drew *you-know-who*. You can bet she knows I'm an artist now!"

"YAY!!!" cheered the kids.

"So, to answer your question"— Jim smiled—"the best part of making books is coming up with the perfect ending."

THE LAST STORY

THE HOSPITAL

James Marshall was very sick.

"Do you think they'll remember me, Mama?" asked Jim.

"We all will," said his mother. "Your father and I, your sister, your nephew and niece."

"That's good," said Jim. "Anyone else?"

"Well, there's Maurice, of course," said his mother.

"Lovely, loyal Maurice," said Jim.

"And Billy," said his father.

Jim smiled.

"And the kids," added his father. "Your readers—they will remember you."

"Will you tell them where I've gone?" asked Jim.

"I don't think I can," said Jim's mother.

"That's all right," said Jim. "They'll figure it out . . ."

"Kids are really smart these days."

Taken by William Gray in 1979 in Saratoga with a 105mm portrait lens on film; used with permission

AUTHOR'S NOTE

JAMES EDWARD MARSHALL was born on October 10, 1942 in San Antonio, Texas. He was known as Jim to his friends. I call him both "James Marshall" and "Jim" in this book because while I didn't know him personally, I feel like I understand the story of his life and work. That's why I wanted to write this book.

I decided to draw Jim as a fox because of all the characters he created, Fox (from *Fox and His Friends*) is the one he said was most like him.

In fact, I have put many Marshall references in this book. Did you see his two hippos, George and Martha, hiding anywhere? I wonder how many of these secrets you will find.

I tried to stay true to a James Marshall feeling in my drawings, but I did change one thing. Jim used Native American headdresses as a costume in many of his illustrations. You will see them in stories about Halloween, dress-up, or masquerade balls. I think using someone else's tradition is hurtful to the person you are taking the tradition from, so

on page 65 where there are kids playing outside, I outfitted one of them in something more true to Jim's own heritage. He was always proud of his Texas roots, so I think that was a good choice.

I won't give away all the book's secrets, but here are few more details you might find interesting.

STORY NUMBER ONE
THE BOOK

James Marshall met Harry Allard at Trinity College, where Harry taught French. Together they wrote ten books. Harry enjoyed stories with strange settings and even stranger characters. Jim liked Harry's ideas but he knew they had to be made appropriate for picture books. Jim did a lot of work to shape Harry's words, but he was always happy to give his friend top billing.

Miss Nelson Is Missing! wasn't the first book they wrote together, but it was definitely the most popular.

STORY NUMBER TWO
"HOW CUTE!"

James Marshall really did not like it when people called his work "cute" or "zany." He created his books at a time when illustrators who drew in a cartoony style weren't always considered true artists. This was very frustrating to Jim. Showing off his skill as a classical musician was a way to let people know he was serious about fine art.

James Marshall was in an airplane flying to a classical music competition in Puerto Rico but it never crashed. It *did* have a really rough landing and he *did* hurt his wrist a little, but the story is mostly an exaggeration.

STORY NUMBER THREE
FRIENDLY COMPETITION

James Marshall, Maurice Sendak (creator of *Where the Wild Things Are*), and Arnold Lobel (creator of the Frog and Toad series) really were friends and they really did go on adventures together. One time, the three friends were goofing around at a fancy opera. That was when Anita Lobel, an author and illustrator herself, first started calling them "Cutups" (a cutup is a person who can't help making jokes when they're supposed to be serious).

Of the three, Jim and Maurice were best friends. Maurice was a little older than Jim, and Jim took Maurice's opinion very seriously. Maurice considered James Marshall to be the most honest and funniest children's book creator of his time but he also knew that because Jim made his drawings look so simple, people would think they were easy.

There was nothing to be done about that. Few people knew as well as Maurice how hard Jim worked at getting his books just right. He often wished more people took Jim's work as seriously as he did.

STORY NUMBER FOUR
THE AWARD

James Marshall knew the best way to be taken seriously would be to win an award. Jim won

JAMES MARSHALL TIMELINE →

1942	1950	1953	1959	1961	1965	1970	1971
Born in San Antonio, Texas	Age six, decides to stop drawing after being told his drawing of a tree isn't very good	Starts playing viola	Attends music camp for viola in Interlochen, Michigan	Flies to Puerto Rico and "hurts hand" in rough landing	Begins drawing again	First job as an illustrator for *Plink Plink Plink* by Byrd Baylor	Doodles two hippos while lying in a hammock

a second place for a very important illustration award (he received the Caldecott Honor in 1989 for *Goldilocks and the Three Bears*). Jim was proud but secretly he wished for first place.

The drawing of Jim and Billy in their bedroom is a reference to an illustration in Marshall's version of *The Night Before Christmas*. In the original illustration, Billy's face is hidden behind a sleep mask.

James Marshall was gay. He and his partner Billy loved each other very much. His friends and his publishers knew he was gay and so did his family. But at this time, being gay wasn't something that was easy to talk about. Still, Jim was able to express himself through his art. The painting on pages 42–43 is based on Jim's picture book *The Owl and the Pussy-cat,* which he dedicated to Billy.

STORY NUMBER FIVE
THE SCHOOL VISIT

James Marshall did draw a picture of a pecan tree in second grade and his teacher did tell him he wouldn't be an artist. This unnamed teacher was the inspiration for Viola Swamp in the Miss Nelson books.

THE LAST STORY
THE HOSPITAL

James Marshall died of a condition called AIDS on October 13, 1992. Medication for AIDS was new and still being developed and people were often too scared to talk about it. For a long time, many people believed James Marshall died of a brain tumor.

"Lovely, loyal Maurice" were Jim's last words to his best friend.

"Kids are really smart these days" is a line from Marshall's *Fox All Week* and it's something I know Jim believed.

In all of his books, James Marshall spoke to kids with respect. He trusted that kids would understand his jokes. I hope you understand why I wanted to tell you Jim's life story.

1972	1977	1977	1978	1982	1984	1989	1992	1998
George and Martha published	Meets Bill Gray, who he comes to call Billy	*Miss Nelson is Missing!* published, text by Harry Allard	Moves to Connecticut	Makes mischief at the opera with Maurice and Arnold in New York City	*The Cut-Ups* published	Wins Caldecott Honor for *Goldilocks and the Three Bears*	Dies in New York City	Final book, *The Owl and the Pussycat,* publishes